Garden Beauty... Q

pieced by Donna Arends Hansen
quilted by Julie Lawson

One of the reasons I love Quilt of the Month quilts is that every block is different, so every square offers new and exciting patterns as well as opportunities to practice a variety of piecing skills.

Block of the Month projects become even more fun when shared with groups of friends. Quilters have a long history of gathering together for piecing and quilting, conversation and company. The sometimes daunting task of making a large quilt becomes an exciting opportunity to share news and it's amazing how quickly and pleasantly the project moves forward when you sew with friends.

I hope this quilt inspires you to gather your group and experience the joys of quilting.

Suzanne

Fabric collections can often be purchased in 'Jelly Roll' bundles of coordinating colors and prints.

Your private stash of assorted fabrics is also a wonderful source for 'scrappy quilts'.

Cut fabric with a sharp rotary cutter, a quilter's ruler and a self-healing cutting mat.

PHOTOS ARE ON PAGES 2, 19 AND 20.

SIZE: 58" x 74"

YARDAGE:

We used a *Moda* "Portugal" by April Cornell
'Jelly Roll' collection of 2½" fabric strips
- we purchased 1 'Jelly Roll'

⅔ yard Creamy Yellow	OR	9 strips
¾ yard Golden Yellow	OR	10 strips
⅝ yard Coral Red	OR	8 strips
½ yard Blue	OR	6 strips
⅓ yard Green	OR	4 strips

Border #1	Purchase ½ yard Red
Border #2 & Binding	Purchase 1⅞ yards Blue
Backing	Purchase 3½ yards
Batting	Purchase 66" x 82"
Sewing machine, needle, thread	

Fabric is from Moda / United Notions
www.unitednotions.com

Garden Beauty

11 different Blocks plus the Border

Design Originals For a color catalog featuring over 200 terrific 'How-To' books, **visit www.d-originals.com**

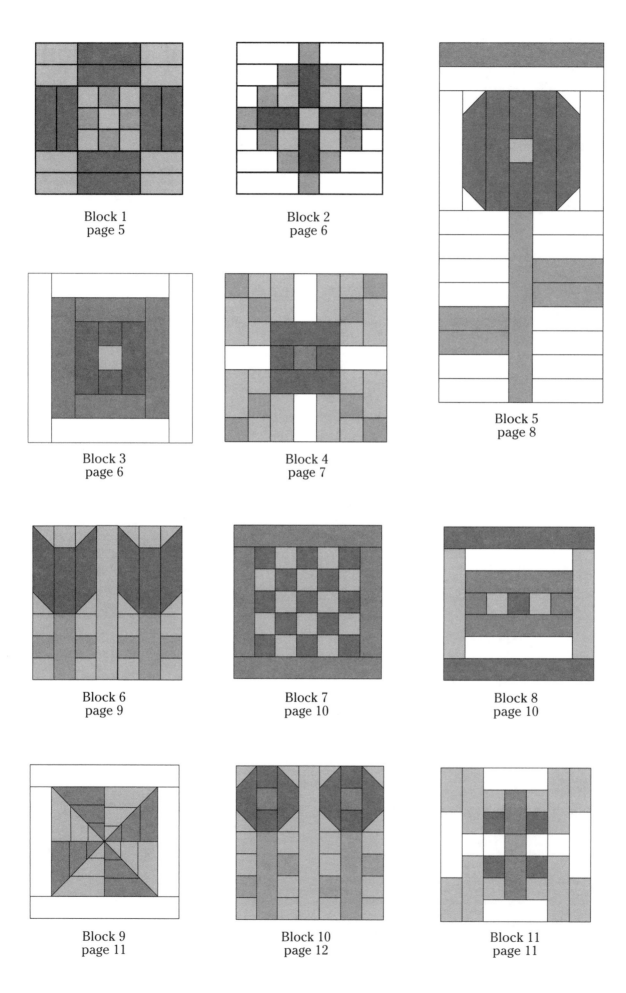

Block 1
page 5

Block 2
page 6

Block 3
page 6

Block 4
page 7

Block 5
page 8

Block 6
page 9

Block 7
page 10

Block 8
page 10

Block 9
page 11

Block 10
page 12

Block 11
page 11

Garden Beauty
Quilt of the Month

SIZE: 58" x 74"

PREPARATION:

TIP: All strips are 2½" wide. Label the pieces as you cut.

TIP: You may need to sew smaller strips end to end to enable you to cut a longer piece. This adds to the charm of the scrappy look.

Unit A - Corners

BLOCK 1:

Unit A - Corners:

Cut 2 Golden Yellow strips 18" long.
Sew the strips together to make a piece 4½" x 18".
Cut the piece into 4 units 4½" x 4½".

Unit B - Sides

Unit B - Sides:

Cut 2 Red strips 26" long.
Sew the strips together to make a piece 4½" x 26".
Cut the piece into 4 units 4½" x 6½".

Top Row

Unit C - Checkerboard Center:

Top Row:

Cut 2 Golden Yellow squares 2½" x 2½".
Cut 1 Green square 2½" x 2½".
Sew the 3 squares together as Gold - Green - Gold.

Bottom Rows

Bottom Rows:

Cut 1 Golden Yellow strip and 1 Green strip 7½" long.
Sew the 2 strips together side by side to 4½" x 7½".
Cut into 3 sections 2½" x 4½" (2 colors in each section).

Assemble Bottom Rows:

Arrange the 2-color sections following the diagram.
Sew the 3 sections together. Press.

Unit C - Checkerboard

Assemble Checkerboard Center:

Sew the Top row and Bottom rows together. Press.

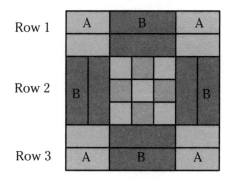

Block 1

BLOCK 1 ASSEMBLY:

Follow the Block #1 Assembly Diagram.

Rows 1 & 3:

Sew a Unit A to each side of a Unit B. Press.

Row 2:

Sew a Unit B to each side of the Unit C Checkerboard. Press.

Assemble:

Sew the rows together. Press.

BLOCK 2:

CUTTING CHART:

Creamy Yellow

Quantity	Length	Position
4	6½"	Rows 1
4	4½"	Rows 2
4	2½"	Rows 3

Blue

4	4½"	Center Row & Center Column

Green

12	2½"	Rows 2, 3, Center & Center Row

Golden Yellow

5	2½"	Rows 3 & Center

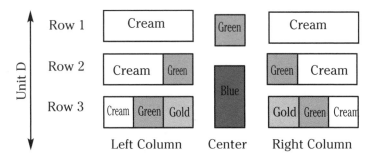

PREPARATION FOR BLOCK 2

Row Strips:

Row 1: Use a Cream 6½" strip

Row 2: Sew a Cream 4½" to a Green 2½". Press. Make 4.

Row 3: Sew the following 2½" squares:
Cream-Green-Gold. Press. Make 4.

Assemble Columns:

Left: Sew Rows 1, 2 and 3 together side by side. Press. Make 2.

Right: Note the position of colors in the strips.
Sew Rows 1, 2 and 3 together side by side. Press. Make 2.

Center: Sew Green 2½" square to Blue 4½" strip. Press. Make 2.

Assemble Unit D:

Sew Left Column to Center to Right Column. Press. Make 2.

Center Row:

Sew a Green 2½" - Blue 4½" - Gold 2½" - Blue 4½" - Green 2½".
Press.

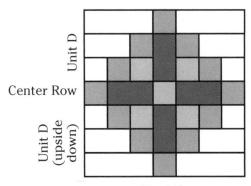

Block 2

BLOCK 2 ASSEMBLY:

Arrange the pieces following the Block Assembly diagram.
Sew Unit D to Center Row to Unit D (upside down). Press.

BLOCK 3:

CUTTING CHART:

Creamy Yellow

Quantity	Length	Position
2	14½"	#12, #13
2	10½"	#10, #11

Golden Yellow

1	2½"	#1

Red

2	6½"	#4, #5
2	2½"	#2, #3

Blue

2	10½"	#8, #9
2	6½"	#6, #7

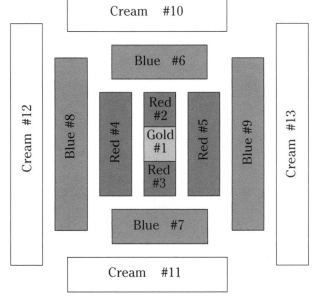

Block 3 - Sections Diagram

BLOCK ASSEMBLY:

Sew a Red square #2 and #3 to each end of Gold #1.
Press. Make 1.

Sew Red #4 and Red #5 to the sides of #1-2-3. Press.

Sew Blue #6 and Blue #7 to the top and bottom of
#1-2-3-4-5. Press.

Sew Blue #8 and #9 to the sides of the piece. Press.

Sew Cream #10 and #11 to the top and bottom of
the piece. Press.

Sew Cream #12 and #13 to the sides of the piece.
Press.

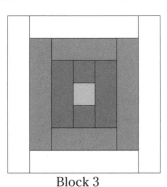

Block 3

BLOCK 4:

CUTTING CHART:

Creamy Yellow

Quantity	Length	Position
1	8½"	#4
1	9"	#5
2	4½"	#7

Golden Yellow

4	4½"	#2
2	10"	#3
2	9"	#6

Red

2	6½"	#10
2	2½"	#8

Green

4	2½"	#1
1	10"	#4

Blue

1	2½"	#9

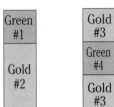
Unit #1

Unit #2

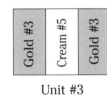
Unit #3

Unit #1:
Sew Green #1 to Gold #2 to make a piece 2½" x 6½". Press. Make 4. (2 for Section A and 2 for Section C).

Unit #2:
Sew Gold #3, Green #4 and Gold #3 together side by side to make a piece 6½" x 10". Press.
Cut the piece into 4 units, each 2½" x 6½" (2 for Section A and 2 for Section C).

Unit #3:
Sew Gold #6, Cream #5 and Gold #6 together side by side to make a piece 6½" x 9". Press.
Cut the piece into 2 units, each 4½" x 6½"

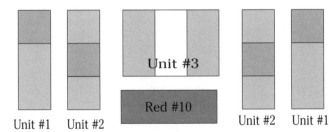

Unit #1 Unit #2   Unit #2 Unit #1

Section A   Section B   Section C

PREPARATION FOR BLOCK 4:

Section A:
Sew Unit #1 to Unit #2. Press. Make 2.

Section B:
Note the position of the units.
Sew Unit #1 to Unit #2. Press. Make 2

Section C:
Sew Red #10 to the bottom of Unit #3. Press. Make 2.

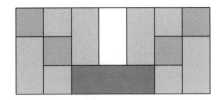
Section D

Section D:
Refer to the diagram for position and direction of the pieces.
Sew Section A to Section B to Section C. Press. Make 2.

Cream #7	Red #8	Blue #9	Red #8	Cream #7

Center Row

Center Row:
Sew the following together end to end: #7 - #8 - #9 - #8 - #7. Press.

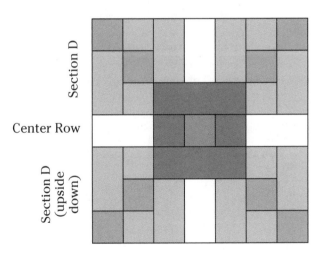

Block 4
Assembly Diagram

BLOCK ASSEMBLY:
Refer to the Block Assembly diagram and arrange sections and rows as shown.
Sew Section D to the Center Row to another Section D (upside down). Press.

BLOCK 5:

CUTTING CHART:

Blue

Quantity	Length	Position
1	14½"	Blue Sky

Creamy Yellow

1	14½"	Flower top border
2	10½"	Flower side borders
4	2½"	Flower corners
6	13"	Leaf section

Red

4	10½"	Flower
2	4½"	Flower

Green

1	16½"	Stem
2	13"	Leaf section

Golden Yellow

1	2½"	Flower center

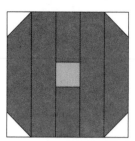

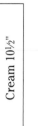

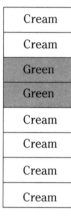

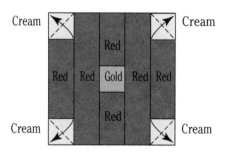

Folded Corners Diagram
for Snowball Flower

Leaf Section   Stem   Leaf Section
(upside down)

PREPARATION FOR BLOCK 5:

Flower:

Center Column:

Sew a Red 4½" strip to each end of the Gold 2½" square. Press.

Sew 2 Red 10½" strips to each side of this center piece to make a 10½" square. Press.

Add Snowball Corners:

Align a Cream 2½" square with each corner.

Noting the direction, draw a diagonal line in each square.

Sew on the diagonal as shown.

Fold back Cream squares to form corner triangles.

Trim away excess fabric underneath the flower.

Add Additional Strips:

Sew a Cream 10½" strip to each side of the flower. Press.

Sew a Cream 14½" strip to the top. Press.

Sew a Blue 14½" strip to the top. Press.

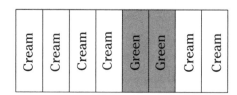

Cut 13" x 16½"
into two pieces
6½" x 16½"

Stem and Leaf Section:

Refer to diagram for position of Leaf Sections.

Sew sections together:

Leaf Section - Green 16½" stem - Leaf Section. Press.

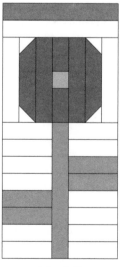

Block 5

Leaf Sections:

Sew 13" strips together side by side in the following order:

4 Cream - 2 Green - 2 Cream to make a piece 13" x 16½". Press.

Cut the piece into 2 sections, each 6½" x 16½".

BLOCK ASSEMBLY:

Sew the Snowball Flower section to the Stem and Leaf section. Press.

BLOCK 6:

CUTTING CHART:

Red

Quantity	Length	Position
4	8½"	Flower sides
2	6½"	Flower center

Green

1	10"	Leaf Section
2	6½"	Stem

Golden Yellow

1	14½"	Sashing
10	2½"	Flower center and corners
2	10"	Leaf Section

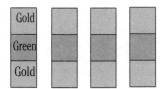

Cut 4 Leaf Sections   Stem

Leaf Sections:
Sew strips together side by side:
Gold 10" - Green 10" - Gold 10".
Press.
Cut piece into 4 sections, each 2½" x 6½".

Leaf   Stem   Leaf
Section   Section

Stem & Leaf Sections:
Sew sections together side by side:
Leaf Section - Stem - Leaf Section.
Press. Make 2.

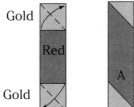    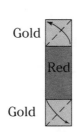 

Flower Side A   Flower Side B

Flower Side A:
Align a Gold square to each end of a Red 6½" strip. Press.
Noting the direction, draw a diagonal line in each square.
Sew on the diagonal as shown.
Fold back the Gold triangles. Press. Make 2 of side A.
Trim away excess fabric underneath.

Flower Side B:
Repeat the instructions as above.
NOTE: The diagonal corners are opposite directions.
Make 2 of side B.

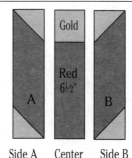

Side A   Center   Side B

Flower Section

Center of Flowers:
Sew a Gold square to the end of a Red 6½" strip.
Press. Make 2.

Flower Sections:
Sew a Side A, Center and Side B together side by side.
Press. Make 2.

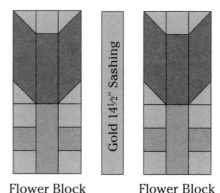

Flower Block   Flower Block

Flower Block:
Sew Flower Sections to Stem Sections.
Press. Make 2.

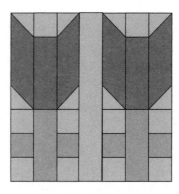

Block 6

BLOCK ASSEMBLY:
Sew blocks and sashing together side by side:
Flower Block - Sashing - Flower Block.
Press.

Block 7:

CUTTING CHART:

Golden Yellow

Quantity	Length	Position
2	7½"	Unit A
3	5"	Unit B

Red

3	7½"	Unit A
2	5"	Unit B

Blue

2	14½"	Top and Bottom borders
2	10½"	Side borders

Unit A

Unit B

PREPARATION FOR BLOCK 7:

Unit A for Rows 1, 3 & 5:
Sew 7½" strips together side by side to make 7½" x 10½":
Red - Gold - Red - Gold - Red. Press.
Cut this piece into 3 sections 2½" x 10½". Label these "A".

Unit B for Rows 2 & 4:
Sew 5" strips together side by side to make 5" x 10½":
Gold - Red - Gold - Red - Gold. Press.
Cut this piece into 2 sections 2½" x 10½". Label these "B".

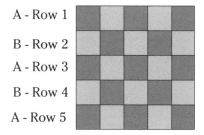

A - Row 1
B - Row 2
A - Row 3
B - Row 4
A - Row 5

Checkerboard

Checkerboard:
Arrange the rows in the following order: A - B - A - B - A.
Sew the rows together. Press.

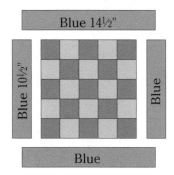

Blue 14½"

Blue 10½"

Blue

Blue

Assembly Diagram

Block 7

BLOCK ASSEMBLY:
Refer to the Block Assembly diagram.
Sew Blue 10½" strips to the right and left sides of block. Press.
Sew Blue 14½" strips to the top and bottom of block. Press.

Block 8:

CUTTING CHART:

Creamy Yellow

Quantity	Length	Position
2	10½"	#8, #9

Red

2	14½"	#12, #13

(Tip: Choose the lightest Reds for these positions to get a good contrast with the Dark Red sashing)

1	2½"	#3

Golden Yellow

2	10½"	#10, #11
2	2½"	#2, #4

Blue

2	10½"	#6, #7
2	2½"	#1, #5

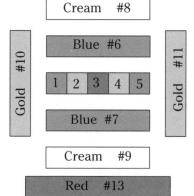

Assembly Diagram

BLOCK ASSEMBLY:
Sew squares together for the center:
Blue #1 - Gold #2 - Red #3 - Gold #4 - Blue #5.
Press.
Sew Blue #6 and #7 to the top and bottom.
Press.
Sew Cream #8 and #9 to the top and bottom.
Press.
Sew Gold #10 and #11 to the sides.
Press.
Sew Red #12 and #13 to the top and bottom .
Press.

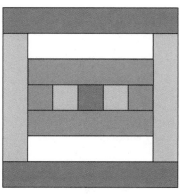

Block 8

Block 9:

CUTTING CHART

Creamy Yellow

Quantity	Length	Position
2	10½"	Side borders
2	14½"	Top and Bottom borders

Golden Yellow

Quantity	Length	Position
3	13"	Center pinwheel

Blue

Quantity	Length	Position
3	13"	Center pinwheel

Gold 13"   Blue 13"

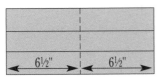

PREPARATION FOR BLOCK 9:

Sew 3 Gold strips together side by side to make 6½" x 13". Press. Cut the piece in 2 squares 6½" x 6½".
Sew 3 Blue strips together side by side to make 6½" x 13". Press. Cut the piece in 2 squares 6½" x 6½".

Each pair of Blue/Gold squares makes 2 Half-Square Triangle blocks

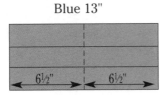

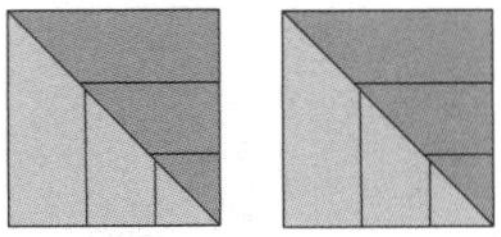

HALF-SQUARE TRIANGLES:

TIP: Refer to Half-Square Triangle instructions on page 15.
Pair up a 6½" Blue and a 6½" Gold square.
Draw a line from corner to corner on the diagonal.
Sew a seam ¼" on each side of the diagonal line.
Cut apart on the diagonal line to make 2 squares. Press.
Make 4 Half-Square Triangles.
Center and trim each Half-Square Triangle to 5½" x 5½".

ASSEMBLE A PINWHEEL:

TIP: It is not necessary to match the interior seams.
Arrange 4 half-square triangles in a Pinwheel.
Sew 2 rows of 2 blocks. Press.
Sew the rows together. Press.

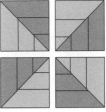

Pinwheel Block

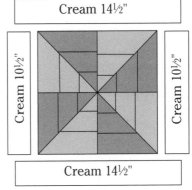

Cream 14½"

Cream 10½"   Cream 10½"

Cream 14½"

Assembly Diagram

ASSEMBLE BLOCK 9:

Sew 10½" Cream strips to the right and left sides of the block. Press.
Sew 14½" Cream strips to the top and bottom of the block. Press.

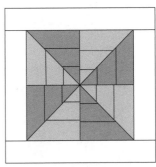

Block 9

Block 11:

CUTTING CHART:

Creamy Yellow

Quantity	Length	Position
4	6½"	#2

Golden Yellow

Quantity	Length	Position
4	6½"	#6
4	4½"	#1
4	2½"	#4

Blue

Quantity	Length	Position
2	4½"	#5
1	10½"	#7

Red

Quantity	Length	Position
4	2½"	#3

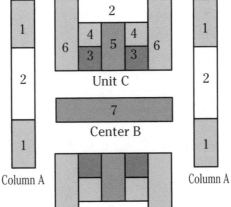

Column A

Unit C

Center B

Unit C (upside down)

Column A

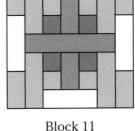

Block 11

PREPARATION FOR BLOCK 11:

Column A: Sew Gold #1 - Cream #2 - Gold #1. Press. Make 2.
Center B: Use a 10½" Blue #7.
Unit C: D: Sew Gold #4 to Red #3. Make 4. Press.
E: Sew a D to each side of Blue #5. Make 2. Press.
F: Sew a Cream #2 top of E. Make 2. Press.
G: Sew a Gold #6 to each side of F. Make 2. Press.

ASSEMBLE BLOCK 11:

Sew Unit C to Center B to Unit C (upside down) to make the center section. Press.
Sew a Column A to each side. Press.

Block 10:

CUTTING CHART:

Golden Yellow

Quantity	Length	Position
1	14½"	Sashing between the flowers
8	2½"	Folded corners
3	10"	Leaf sections

Red

4	6½"	Flower
4	2½"	Flower center strip

Blue

2	2½"	Flower center

Green

2	8½"	Stem
1	10"	Leaf sections

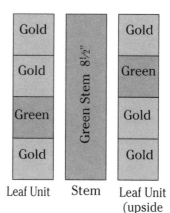

Leaf Unit   Stem   Leaf Unit (upside down)

Leaf & Stem Section

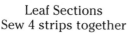

Leaf Sections
Sew 4 strips together

Cut into 4
Leaf Units.

Leaf & Stem Sections:
Note position of the Green leaves on the Leaf Units.
> Sew sections together side by side:
> Leaf Unit - Stem - Leaf Unit (upside down)
> Press. Make 2.

Leaf Sections:
> Sew 10" strips together side by side in the following order:
> Gold - Gold - Green - Gold.
> Press.
> Cut the piece into 4 Leaf Units, each 2½" x 8½".

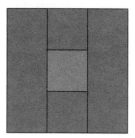

Snowball Flower Strips

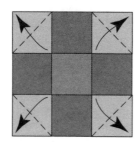

Sew and Fold the Corners

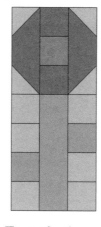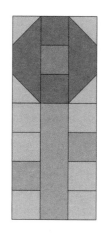

Gold Sashing 14½"

Flower Sections:
> Sew a Flower Block to a Leaf & Stem Section.
> Press. Make 2.

Assemble Block:
> Sew sections together:
> Flower Section - Gold Sashing - Flower Section.
> Press.

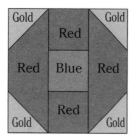

Gold		Gold
	Red	
Red	Blue	Red
	Red	
Gold		Gold

Snowball Flower Block

Snowball Flower Block:

Center Strip: Sew a Red 2½" - Blue 2½" - Red 2½". Press.
Sew a Red 6½" to the right and left sides of the center strip. Press.

Add the Corners:
Refer to the Folded Corners diagram.
Align a Gold 2½" square with each corner.
Noting the direction, draw a diagonal line in each corner square.
Sew on the diagonal. Fold back the Gold squares to form triangles.
Press. Make 2. Trim away excess fabric underneath.

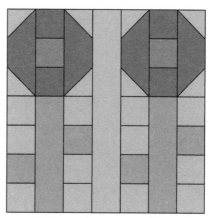

Block 10

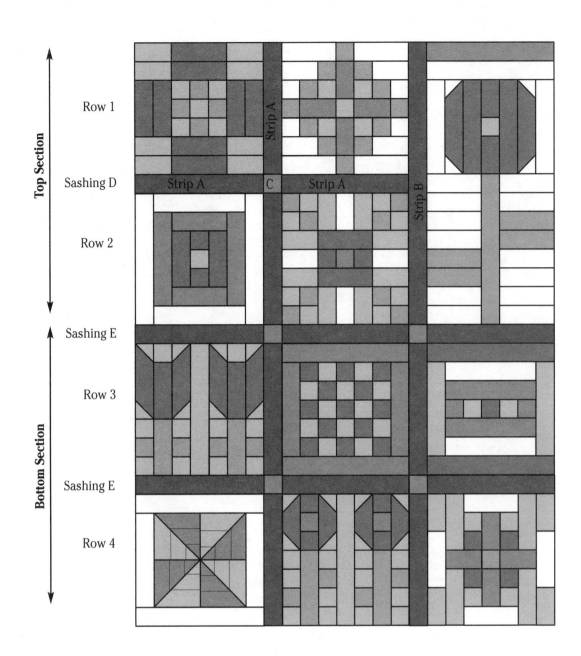

Within the diagram:
- Row 1
- Top Section
- Sashing D
- Strip A
- Strip A
- C
- Strip B
- Row 2
- Sashing E
- Bottom Section
- Row 3
- Sashing E
- Row 4

CUT THE SASHING STRIPS:

Strip A:
Cut 14 strips Red 2½" x 14½" for vertical and horizontal sashing that divides the blocks.

Strip B:
Cut 1 Red strip 2½" x 30½" for vertical sashing next to the large flower block.

Square C:
Cut 5 Blue squares 2½" x 2½" for cornerstones.

PREPARE SASHING STRIPS:

Sashing D: Sew sashing strips together end to end:
Red A - Blue C - Red A.
Press.

Sashing E: Sew sashing strips together end to end:
Red A - Blue C - Red A - Blue C - Red A.
Make 2. Press.

ASSEMBLY:

Arrange all Blocks on a work surface or table.
Refer to diagram for block placement and direction.

Top Section:
Sew Row 1 together:
Block 1 - Red A sashing - Block 2. Press.
Sew Row 2 together:
Block 3 - Red A sashing - Block 4. Press.
Sew Top Section together:
Sew Row 1 - Sashing D - Row 2. Press.
Sew the Red B 30½" sashing to the right side. Press.
Sew Block 5 to the right side. Press.

Bottom Section:
Sew Row 3 together and press:
Block 6 - Red A sashing - Block 7 - Red A sashing - Block 8.
Sew Row 4 together and press:
Block 9 - Red A sashing - Block 10 - Red A sashing - Block 11.
Sew Bottom Section together:
Sew Row 3 - Sashing E - Row 4 together. Press.

Assemble Top and Bottom Sections:
Sew Top Section - Sashing E - Bottom Section together. Press.

Garden Beauty - Quilt Assembly

BORDERS:
Border #1:
   Cut 2 Red strips 2½" x 62½" for sides.
   Cut 2 Red strips 2½" x 50½" for top and bottom.
   Sew side borders to the quilt. Press.
   Sew top and bottom borders to the quilt. Press.

Border #2:
TIP: Cut the strips parallel to the selvage to eliminate piecing
      on the long borders.
   Cut 2 strips 4½" x 66½" for sides.
   Cut 2 strips 4½" x 58½" for top and bottom.
   Sew side borders to the quilt. Press.
   Sew top and bottom borders to the quilt. Press.

FINISHING:
Quilting: See Basic Instructions on pages 15 - 17.
Binding: Cut strips 2½" wide.
         Sew together end to end to equal 274".
         See Binding Instructions on page 15.

Basic Quilting Instructions

Hand Quilting:

Many quilters enjoy the serenity of hand quilting. Because the quilt is handled a great deal, it is important to securely baste the sandwich together. Place the quilt in a hoop and don't forget to hide your knots.

Machine Quilting:

All the quilts in this book were machine quilted. Some were quilted on a large, free-arm quilting machine and others were quilted on a sewing machine. If you have never machine quilted before, practice on some scraps first.

Straight Line Machine Quilting Tips:

1. Pin baste the layers securely.

2. Set up your sewing machine with a size 80 quilting needle and a walking foot.

3. Experimenting with the decorative stitches on your machine adds interest to your quilt. You do not have to quilt the entire piece with the same stitch. Variety is the spice of life, so have fun trying out stitches you have never used before as well as your favorite stand-bys.

Free Motion Machine Quilting Tips:

1. Pin baste the layers securely.

2. Set up your sewing machine with a spring needle, a quilting foot, and lower the feed dogs.

Basic Mitered Binding Instructions

A Perfect Finish:

The binding endures the most stress on a quilt and is usually the first thing to wear out. For this reason, we recommend using a double fold binding.

1. Trim the backing and batting even with the quilt edge.

2. If possible cut strips on the crosswise grain because a little bias in the binding is a Good thing. This is the only place in the quilt where bias is helpful, for it allows the binding to give as it is turned to the back and sewn in place.

3. Strips are usually cut 2½" wide, but check the instructions for your project before cutting.

4. Sew strips end to end to make a long strip sufficient to go all around the quilt plus 4"- 6".

5. With wrong sides together, fold the strip in half lengthwise. Press.

6. Stretch out your hand and place your little finger at the corner of the quilt top. Place the binding where your thumb touches the edge of the quilt. Aligning the edge of the quilt with the raw edges of the binding, pin the binding in place along the first side.

7. Leaving a 2" tail for later use, begin sewing the binding to the quilt with a ¼" seam.

For Mitered Corners:

1. Stop ¼" from the first corner. Leave the needle in the quilt and turn it 90°. Hit the reverse button on your machine and back off the quilt leaving the threads connected.

2. Fold the binding perpendicular to the side you sewed, making a 45° angle. Carefully maintaining the first fold, bring the binding back along the edge to be sewn.

3. Carefully align the edges of the binding with the quilt edge and sew as you did the first side. Repeat this process until you reach the tail left at the beginning. Fold the tail out of the way and sew until you are ¼" from the beginning stitches.

4. Remove the quilt from the machine. Fold the quilt out of the way and match the binding tails together. Carefully sew the binding tails with a ¼" seam. You can do this by hand if you prefer.

Finishing the Binding:

5. Trim the seam to reduce bulk.

6. Finish stitching the binding to the quilt across the join you just sewed.

7. Turn the binding to the back of the quilt. To reduce bulk at the corners, fold the miter in the opposite direction from which it was folded on the front.

8. Hand-sew a Blind stitch on the back of the quilt to secure the binding in place.

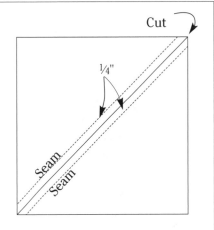

Half-Square Triangle Diagram
1. Place 2 squares right sides together.
2. Draw a diagonal line from corner to corner.
3. Stitch ¼" on each side of the line.
4. Cut squares apart on the diagonal line.
5. Open the 2 new squares with 2 colors.
6. Press. Trim off dog-ears.
7. Center and trim to size.

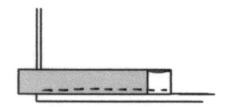

Align the raw edge of the binding with the raw edge of the quilt top. Start about 8" from the corner and go along the first side with a ¼" seam.

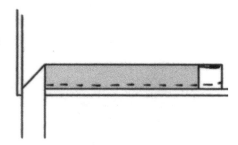

Stop ¼" from the edge. Then stitch a slant to the corner (through both layers of binding)... lift up, then down, as you line up the edge. Fold the binding back.

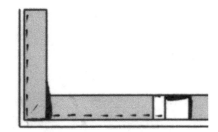

Align the raw edge again. Continue stitching the next side with a ¼" seam as you sew the binding in place.

Tips for Working with Strips

TIPS: As a Guide for Yardage:
Each $1/4$ yard or a 'Fat Quarter' equals 3 strips
A pre-cut 'Jelly Roll' strip is $2^1/2$" x 44"
Cut 'Fat Quarter' strips to $2^1/2$" x 22"

Pre-cut strips are cut on the crosswise grain and are prone to stretching. These tips will help reduce stretching and make your quilt lay flat for quilting.

1. If you are cutting yardage, cut on the grain. Cut fat quarters on grain, parallel to the 18" side.

2. When sewing crosswise grain strips together, take care not to stretch the strips. If you detect any puckering as you go, rip out the seam and sew it again.

3. Press, Do Not Iron. Carefully open fabric, with the seam to one side, press without moving the iron. A back-and-forth ironing motion stretches the fabric.

4. Reduce the wiggle in your borders with this technique from garment making. First, accurately cut your borders to the exact measure of the quilt top. Then, before sewing the border to the quilt, run a double row of stay stitches along the outside edge to maintain the original shape and prevent stretching. Pin the border to the quilt, taking care not to stretch the quilt top to make it fit. Pinning reduces slipping and stretching.

Rotary Cutting Tips

Rotary Cutter: Friend or Foe

A rotary cutter is wonderful and useful. When not used correctly, the sharp blade can be a dangerous tool. Follow these safety tips:
1. Never cut toward you.
2. Use a sharp blade. Pressing harder on a dull blade can cause the blade to jump the ruler and injure your fingers.
3. Always disengage the blade before the cutter leaves your hand, even if you intend to pick it up immediately.

Rotary cutters have been caught when lifting fabric, have fallen onto the floor and have cut fingers.

Basic Sewing Instructions

You now have precisely cut strips that are exactly the correct width. You are well on your way to blocks that fit together perfectly. Accurate sewing is the next important step.

Matching Edges:

1. Carefully line up the edges of your strips. Many times, if the underside is off a little, your seam will be off by $1/8$". This does not sound like much until you have 8 seams in a block, each off by $1/8$". Now your finished block is a whole inch wrong!

2. Pin the pieces together to prevent them shifting.

Seam Allowance:

I cannot stress enough the importance of accurate $1/4$" seams. All the quilts in this book are measured for $1/4$" seams unless otherwise indicated.

Most sewing machine manufacturers offer a Quarter-inch foot. A Quarter-inch foot is the most worthwhile investment you can make in your quilting.

Pressing:

I want to talk about pressing even before we get to

sewing because proper pressing can make the difference between a quilt that wins a ribbon at the quilt show and one that does not.

Press, do NOT iron. What does that mean? Many of us want to move the iron back and forth along the seam. This "ironing" stretches the strip out of shape and creates errors that accumulate as the quilt is constructed. Believe it or not, there is a correct way to press your seams, and here it is:

1. Do NOT use steam with your iron. If you need a little water, spritz it on.

2. Place your fabric flat on the ironing board without opening the seam. Set a hot iron on the seam and count to 3. Lift the iron and move to the next position along the seam. Repeat until the entire seam is pressed. This sets and sinks the threads into the fabric.

3. Now, carefully lift the top strip and fold it away from you so the seam is on one side. Usually the seam is pressed toward the darker fabric, but often the direction of the seam is determined by the piecing requirements.

4. Press the seam open with your fingers. Add a little water or spray starch if it wants to close again. Lift the iron and place it on the seam. Count to 3. Lift the iron again and continue until the seam is pressed. Do NOT use the tip of the iron to push the seam open. So many people do this and wonder later why their blocks are not fitting together.

5. Most critical of all: For accuracy every seam must be pressed before the next seam is sewn.

Working with 'Crosswise Grain' strips:

Strips cut on the crosswise grain (from selvage to selvage) have problems similar to bias edges and are prone to stretching. To reduce stretching and make your quilt lay flat for quilting, keep these tips in mind.

1. Take care not to stretch the strips as you sew.

2. Adjust the sewing thread tension and the presser foot pressure if needed.

3. If you detect any puckering as you go, rip out the seam

and sew it again. It is much easier to take out a seam now than to do it after the block is sewn.

Sewing Bias Edges:

Bias edges wiggle and stretch out of shape very easily. They are not recommended for beginners, but even a novice can accomplish bias edges if these techniques are employed.

1. Stabilize the bias edge with one of these methods:

a) Press with spray starch.

b) Press freezer paper or removable iron-on stabilizer to the back of the fabric.

c) Sew a double row of stay stitches along the bias edge and ⅛" from the bias edge. This is a favorite technique of garment makers.

2. Pin, pin, pin! I know many of us dislike pinning, but when working with bias edges, pinning makes the difference between intersections that match and those that do not.

Building Better Borders:

Wiggly borders make a quilt very difficult to finish. However, wiggly borders can be avoided with these techniques.

1. Cut the borders on grain. That means cutting your strips parallel to the selvage edge.

2. Accurately cut your borders to the exact measure of the quilt.

3. If your borders are piece stripped from crosswise grain fabrics, press well with spray starch and sew a double row of stay stitches along the outside edge to maintain the original shape and prevent stretching.

4. Pin the border to the quilt, taking care not to stretch the quilt top to make it fit. Pinning reduces slipping and stretching.

Basic Layering Instructions

Marking Your Quilt:

If you choose to mark your quilt for hand or machine quilting, it is much easier to do so before layering. Press your quilt before you begin. Here are some handy tips regarding marking.

1. A disappearing pen may vanish before you finish.

2. Use a White pencil on dark fabrics.

3. If using a washable Blue pen, remember that pressing may make the pen permanent.

Pieced Backings:

1. Press the backing fabric before measuring.

2. If possible cut backing fabrics on grain, parallel to the selvage edges.

3. Piece 3 parts rather than 2 whenever possible, sewing 2 side borders to the center. This reduces stress on the pieced seam.

4. The backing and batting should extend at least 2" on each side of the quilt.

Creating a Quilt Sandwich:

1. Press the backing and top to remove all wrinkles.

2. Lay the backing wrong side up on the table.

3. Position the batting over the backing and smooth out all wrinkles.

4. Center the quilt top over the batting leaving a 2" border all around.

5. Pin the layers together with 2" safety pins positioned a handwidth apart. A grapefruit spoon makes inserting the pins easier. Leaving the pins open in the container speeds up the basting on the next quilt.

Applique Instructions

Basic Turned Edge:

1. Trace pattern onto template plastic.

2. Cut out the shape leaving a scant ¼" fabric border all around and clip the curves.

3. Place the template plastic on the wrong side of the fabric. Spray edges with starch.

4. Press the ⅛" border over the edge of the template plastic with the tip of a hot iron. Press firmly.

5. Remove the template, maintaining the folded edge on the back of the fabric.

6. Position the shape on the quilt and Blindstitch in place.

Basic Needle Turn:

1. Cut out the shape leaving a ¼" fabric border all around.

2. Baste the shapes to the quilt, keeping the basting stitches away from the edge of the fabric.

3. Begin with all areas that are under other layers and work to the topmost layer.

4. For an area no more than 2" ahead of where you are working, trim to ⅛" and clip the curves.

5. Using the needle, roll the edge under and sew tiny Blindstitches to secure.

Using Fusible Web for Iron-on Applique:

1. Trace the pattern onto *Steam a Seam 2* fusible web.

2. Press the patterns onto the wrong side of the fabric.

3. Cut out patterns exactly on the drawn line.

4. Score the web paper with a pin, then remove the paper.

5. Position the fabric, fusible side down, on the quilt. Press with a hot iron following the fusible web manufacturer's instructions.

6. Stitch around the edge by hand.

Optional: Stabilize the wrong side of the fabric with your favorite stabilizer.

Use a size 80 machine embroidery needle. Fill the bobbin with lightweight basting thread and thread the machine with a machine embroidery thread that complements the color being appliqued.

Set your machine for a Zigzag stitch and adjust the thread tension if needed. Use a scrap to experiment with different stitch widths and lengths until you find the one you like best.

Sew slowly.

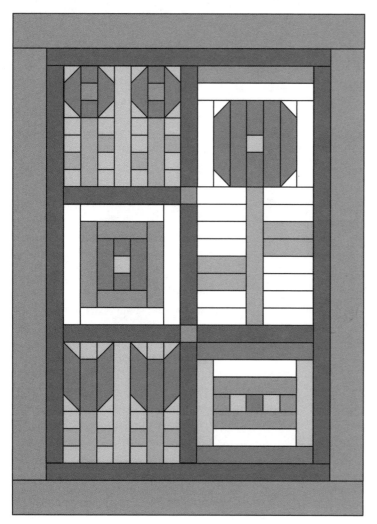

Garden Beauty - Baby Quilt

Baby Quilt Variation

Brighten the nursery with a bold break from the usual pale pastels. These simple shapes and pretty colors will still be welcome as your baby grows from the crib to a child-size bed.

REFER TO INSTRUCTIONS ON PAGES 3 - 17.

SIZE: 42" x 58"

We used 1 Jelly Roll.

TIP: Make a second baby quilt by alternating the leftover fabric and blocks.

YARDAGE:

Border #1	Purchase ⅓ yard
Border #2 & Binding	Purchase 1½ yards
Backing	Purchase 2¾ yards
Batting	Purchase 50" x 66"

Make 1 each of the following:
    Block 3, Block 5, Block 6, Block 8, and Block 10
Cut 6 sashing strips 2½" x 14½".
Cut 2 cornerstones 2½" x 2½".
Assemble as shown.

Border #1:
    Cut 2 strips 2½" x 46½" for sides.
    Cut 2 strips 2½" x 34½" for top and bottom.
Border #2:
    Cut 2 strips 4½" x 50½" for sides.
    Cut 2 strips 4½" x 42½" for top and bottom.
Binding:
    Cut strips 2½" wide.
    Sew together end to end to equal 210".
    See Binding Instructions on page 15.

The Best Things About *Jelly Rolls*

Non-Fattening • Sugar Free • No Cholesterol

Basic Instructions for Cutting, Sewing, Layering, Quilting and Binding are on pages 15 - 17.

TIPS: As a Guide for Yardage:
Each ¼ yard or a 'Fat Quarter' equals 3 strips.
A pre-cut 'Jelly Roll' strip is 2½" x 44".
Cut 'Fat Quarter' and yardage strips to 2½" x 20".

Yardage is given for using either 'Jelly Roll' strips or fabric yardage.

Supplier - Most quilt and fabric stores carry an excellent assortment of supplies. If you need something special, ask your local store to contact the following companies.

FABRICS, 'JELLY ROLLS', 'FAT QUARTERS'
  Moda and United Notions, Dallas, TX, 972-484-8901

QUILTERS
  Julie Lawson, 817-428-5929
  Sue Needle, 817-589-1168

MANY THANKS to my staff for their cheerful help and wonderful ideas!
Kathy Mason • Patty Williams • Janet Long • David & Donna Thomason
Donna Kinsey for skillfully and patiently editing the instructions in this book